Foreword

"The greatest fear that everyone has is that when they stand up to give a speech, their mind will sit down!" ~ Jim Rohn

Anyone can be a master maestro of communication. By using the teaching tools in <u>Speaking From The Heart</u>, you will begin to understand what creates a fear of public speaking and how to overcome it. This book will teach you how to take your insights, crystallize them, and present them to an audience. You will build self-confidence and achieve new results in an effortless process.

Straight from his heart, Jim Turrell teaches—concisely—how to articulate your experiences in a positive and persuasive manner. Almost instantly, you will learn to share from your heart...directly to the heart of your audience. This course will make you feel better about yourself, your audience, your results, and your life in general. <u>Speaking From The Heart</u> will take you from where you are, to where you want to be, on the speaking platform!

-- *Mark Victor Hansen*

Introduction

One time through. That's all it will take to convince you that *Public Speaking from the Heart* has accomplished something marvelous--proving, beyond a doubt, that you can speak with total confidence while you utterly enjoy the entire process.

Just imagine, for example, preparing a talk in 45 minutes or less, and having the complete freedom to speak without notes... never having to look for another joke to tell, yet be remarkably humorous... or for your close, bringing your audience back to your original idea, ending naturally like it was the end of a meal and everyone was full and satisfied... knowing that every word was actually yours, real, authentic, natural, eliminating worry and stress, reducing imitation while strengthening the originality and content of your message.

Public Speaking from the Heart is a collection of stimulating exercises — from *Personal Felt Needs* to *Intuitively Led Research* — in a single, convenient book that promises to be an awakening for speakers like you and me who want great original talks without the worry and fear of failing to deliver our intended message.

An approach like *Public Speaking from the Heart* doesn't "spring to life" overnight. It is the product of more than fifteen years of experience and four years of research. I have carefully reviewed and tested many exercises that will help you focus, organize and integrate ideas, selecting the best of the best. Some are uncomplicated, while others are probing, helping you, the speaker, to clarify, tighten and develop your message, and adding depth and dimension in simple yet effective ways.

Public Speaking from the Heart is not only for speeches, it is remarkably adaptable to training sessions, seminars, and lesson plans. There are over 150 pages of easy to understand explanations and exercises — user friendly, immediately useful, and waiting for you in *Public Speaking from the Heart.*

If you're having a hard time believing this model for presentations can be so thorough yet so easy to learn, don't take my word for it. Listen to your own heart. As you read through the lessons, your heart will begin to reveal, create and, best of all, speak.

Jim Turrell

Public Speaking from the Heart

For information about workshops and classes concerning this book please contact Jim Turrell at (949) 642-1985.

First Printing 1998

ISBN 0-9667986-0-0

HEARTTALK
PUBLICATIONS
(949) 642-1985

CONTENTS

1

Creating
Vital
Topics

Within the heart of every person there is a field of pure potentiality, and a doorway through which the originality and genius of each voice can pass. Once the door is open, the gift of what you know can be given. To open the door, however, you must have the key. Topics are keys that open hearts and stimulate fresh ideas.

Topics represent the focal point of a HeartTalk. Without a core subject, a speaker can wander, losing focus of what is central to her message. Topics function as hubs from which ideas flow outward, propelled by a speaker's need for clarification, confidence and guidance. Topics that come from the heart have the strength of passion because they represent what speakers feel and know to be of primary importance.

Topics that come from the Heart have the strength of Passion

Topics are directly connected to the problems, dreams and curiosities of the speaker. They mirror the core beliefs of the speaker. Topics must be examined and then distilled into the human common de-

7

nominator of the heart: feelings. Many speakers tend to steer clear of heart-feelings that can lead to the unknown—the place listeners secretly hope speakers will examine, but where many speakers fear to go. Thus, a *HeartTalk* topic is the key to opening the unknown, making it possible to examine the subject.

The most effective topics come from within speakers themselves. However, if a topic is assigned, you can still abstract a powerful thematic idea by applying the following exercises.

Topic Exercise One

To tap into your feelings - the thematic center of a HeartTalk. Answer the following questions. Take a sheet of paper. Give yourself three minutes per question and write as much as comes to your mind. Your answers are the raw material from which your thematic focus will flow.

1. What are your most immediate problems—the ones you need to solve as soon as possible? Examples: The garage door needs to be fixed and I'm tired of opening it by hand. Bills are unpaid; I need to make more money. I'm lonely.

2. What are the most important things you dream of? Examples: I dream of living on a 50' sailboat; having the perfect partner; playing par golf.

3. What do you most want to learn or explore, e.g., speak Spanish or Italian; explore Paris or the South Pacific; learn more creative writing techniques.

If the topic is assigned, ask yourself:

1. When it comes to the topic of _____ the most pressing problems that need to be solved are...

2. When it comes to the topic of _____ I dream...

3. When it comes to the topic of _____ the thing I want to learn more about or explore is...

Topic Exercise Two

Once you complete the previous exercise, review the details of your problems, dreams and curiosities. Take a sheet of paper. Identify and record the feelings stimulated by these thoughts. To identify your core beliefs, recombine the details of your problems, dreams, and curiosities with the feelings they have stimulated. Then, complete this statement: If that is the way I feel about this, then I must believe _____.

Your answer will indicate some of the core beliefs that control your thoughts and reactions. Reduce these core beliefs into topics by blending them with your other core beliefs, feelings, and details. If your topic is assigned, follow the same procedure and use your distilled topic as a subtopic. This will be of immeasurable assistance in focusing and developing your ideas. Every HeartTalk has a thematic focal point.

1. Briefly identify the feelings your problems, dreams and curiosities stimulate...
   Examples: frustration, fatigue, worry,
   loneliness, freedom.

2. Complete this statement: If this is how I
   feel about this, then I must believe
   _____ about it.
   Examples: "Breakdowns are always frus-
   trating." "Dreams are hard to demonstrate." "Money is important when I don't
   have any."

3. Create topics by mixing words that represent feelings with words that represent
   details/facts... Examples: Breakdowns,
   Freedom and Goals ~ The Worried
   Dream ~ The Mistaken Cause To Money.

Summary

The examples shown in the previous exercises are the data of life distilled into centralized themes. When you identify problems, dreams, and/or curiosities, you gain access to the feelings each detail is stimulating. To create relevant topics, blend the information from Exercise One with the feelings and other core beliefs in Exercise Two. Mentally combining these elements will prompt the appearance of thematic subject matter linked directly to the heart of the speaker. HeartTalk topics centralize your thinking and help to stimulate further investigation—giving birth to a genuine interest in what you have to say.

Speakers who try to create topics not directly related to themselves never gain access to the heart. Topics are not intended for audiences to always understand. Topics are only important to the speaker because they represent the core feelings, reactions and concepts of her message. For the purpose of providing examples throughout the rest of this book, I have chosen the topic *Breakdowns, Freedom and Goals*. Don't try to relate any meaning to this topic. Its meaning will become more obvious as you work your way through the exercises in this book.

Speaking Out Loud

Speaking Out Loud exercises will be included at the end of each chapter. The purpose is to orally practice your written statements in a relaxed and casual manner. Taking two minutes, stand and talk as if explaining to a friend how you arrived at this topic, and why it is important to you. Share as much detail as you can, but remember to keep talking for two minutes. If in the process you go a little blank, simply be quiet, rethink the details, and continue as words occur to you. The most important component of public speaking is not in what you say, but in the silent thought process from which your words originate.

2

The
Voice
of
Authenticity

A speaker's Voice of Authenticity comes from his ability to be himself in front of an audience. This ability - or speaker's authority - is not difficult to find if one knows where to look. It is that part of a personality that knows where it stands and what it cares about, and the unseen force that delivers a message with the power of personal involvement. The voice of authenticity is a combination of: **Direct Experience** <u>with</u> life; gut-level **Felt Needs** <u>in</u> life; personal **Values and Conflicts** <u>about</u> life and how life appears, in total, to be working or not working.

Speakers who have not yet identified this **Voice** may lack the strength gained through personal experience or reality. Instead, they speak from some other authority. This weakens their messages because they, themselves, are not clearly identified. Listeners crave a voice of authenticity, even if they don't totally agree with the message.

Listeners crave a Voice of Authenticity

How to start

In order to locate your **Voice of Authenticity,** begin by monitoring the motive and intent for what you have to say. HeartTalks communicate what you know and what you care about. When you speak from your heart, you are not seeking approval nor even to persuade. Rather, you are speaking reliably and genuinely—with authenticity.

This authoritative honesty gives your audience maximum freedom to see the importance of what you have to say. Authenticity does not insist that listeners draw any conclusions contrary to what they know, or how they feel.

Authenticity creates an intellectual and emotional position. This allows listeners to weigh the advantages of the speaker's position in comparison to their own, and to freely contrast their own internal logic and feelings to the speaker's. This way, listeners are more likely to draw productive conclusions to serve their own interests. A listener's changed point of view can benefit his future by turning life's direction and/ or the underlying mentality that compels his actions.

For example, if I am sailing a boat and it is my intention to travel from Los Angeles to Hawaii, I must consistently check my position to maintain my course. I cannot assume to safely navigate by simply keeping my compass heading toward what appears to be the right direction. Without frequent checks, I could easily wind up in Australia—because strong and invisible currents may push my boat southwest, despite my correct compass heading. My position is weak, and I am off-course because I lack direct, current, and up-to-date information. Comparatively, a speaker may start out with the intent to communicate a message, but lose the way because no check was made on his personal position in relation to the topic.

Without being in touch with your current and direct life experience, your words can sound weak and off-course, even if they are intellectually correct. Your words need the power, authority, and genuineness of your own internal position—in other words, **Authenticity.**

The three components mentioned at the beginning of this chapter, i.e., <u>Direct Experience</u>; <u>Felt Needs</u>; and <u>Values and Conflicts</u>; will now be examined in order.

Direct Experience

The direct experience of life can only happen in the moment. It is a happening no more than twenty-four hours old. If it is more than twenty-four hours old, it is not direct but, rather, **HISTORY.** This means that direct experience, for the purpose of a HeartTalk, is everything you have newly encountered—emotionally, creatively, intellectually and physically—in the last twenty-four hours. It also includes what you think might be encountered in the *next* twenty-four hours. Anything beyond that time frame tends to become speculative, and wishful thinking. To clarify direct experience, complete the exercise on the next page labeled **Direct Experience**. Read the directions carefully, and make sure you time yourself accordingly; then, move to the following page and continue.

Direct Experience Exercise

Take a sheet of paper. Using the following model, list as much as you can remember about the last twenty-four hours, and what you expect from the next twenty-four hours. When you think of persons you have talked to (or are going to talk to) list their names and move to the next category until you have a least one entry per category. Give yourself about three minutes to do this exercise. If you get stuck and can't think of an answer for a particular category, move on to the next.

Last 24 Hours	Next 24 Hours
1. People	1. People
2. Places	2. Places
3. Conditions	3. Conditions
4. Events	4. Events
5. Feelings	5. Feelings
6. Joyful Experiences	6. Joyful Experiences

Summary

The **Direct Experience** data provide a real-time picture of what is happening in your life. Their importance is in the personal recollection and accounting of what you feel and what appears genuine in the moment.

An important component of a HeartTalk is the ability to motivate the listener to examine the difference between perception and reality. Authenticity mandates that speakers <u>feel</u> this knowledge in order to deliver their messages in a relaxed and casual manner, easily being themselves.

Motivate the listener to examine the difference between Perception and Reality

In a HeartTalk, what you say must always agree with what you feel. People experience fear when speaking in public because they are uncertain of the importance or meaning of what they have to say. To correct this fear, the topic must be connected to the speaker.

Communication from the heart begins with an inherent confidence in knowing oneself as well as one's subject matter. As you gain experience in speaking from your heart, the details of your direct experience become increasingly more symbolic and relevant to your topic.

Felt needs, values and conflicts are always present, even if your memory of the last twenty-four hours was your trip to the grocery store. Everything—from your observations of clerks and other shoppers, to the process of how you pick your produce— mirrors your reasoning and the emotional positions you currently tend to take.

These data represent a direct link to your audience because, they too, wonder if their reality is worthwhile, meaningful, and relevant.

Speaking Out Loud

Take two minutes to stand and orally practice reviewing your direct experience as if your were sharing it with a friend. If you go a little blank, stop and recall more details of the last twenty-four hours and review your anticipation for the next twenty-four. The important thing is to fill the entire two minutes with either reflection or words. One enjoyable addition to this exercise is to recall your sense impressions, through smell, touch, hearing, vision and taste.

Felt Needs

Felt needs are the crux of what causes listeners to remark, "I know what she's talking about." People's collective needs for security, success, acceptance, status, food, shelter, etc. reflect an inner - and often subconscious - emotional memory. These felt needs are a part of deep, compelling

25

currents of commonly-recognized human emotions, and cultural and societal necessities that motivate and influence much of the intention and behavior in most people. We all draw from these streams of transient feelings and desires. Thus, felt needs link the speaker directly to the audience through a commonly-perceived sense of what is important in the reality of the speaker's perception and position (mental posture). Felt needs address what listeners profoundly seek to understand in a variety of ways and at many different levels.

This sea of emotional memory is the same thematic ocean in which we all live, and from which we draw our identities. It is also the place where we find our thematic material for HeartTalk topics. Dealing with one's own felt needs, along with the listener's manner of thinking and feeling, and expressing those attributes from the heart, are powerful and honest declarations of the speaker's true expectations of life.

Felt needs, therefore, reveal an immediate connection to the topic, and carry a powerful moving energy that compels and sometimes dictates the behavior of the speaker and the listener. Felt needs that go unnoticed create hidden agendas in speakers and listeners.

This is the reason communication problems habitually recreate themselves, causing nonproductive talks that result in superficial and temporary changes, e.g., "Sounds good, but it doesn't mean anything."

To identify your felt needs, complete the **Felt Needs** exercise on the following page.

Read the directions carefully and make sure you time yourself accordingly; then, move to the following page and continue.

Felt Needs Exercise

Take a sheet of paper. Write in your topic, and record at least one answer for each question. Give yourself about five minutes to do this exercise. If you get stuck and can't think of an answer, just improvise. (Author's sample topic: Breakdowns, Freedom and Goals)

1. When it comes to the topic of _____, the most pressing problems needing to be solved are . . . <u>Example</u>: *How to handle failures and expectations.*

2. When it comes to the topic of _____, I visualize a positive image of . . .

   <u>Example</u>: *Being free enough to accomplish my goals.*

3. When it comes to the topic of _____, the thing I want to learn more about or explore is . . . <u>Example</u>: *What it means and feels like to be free.*

Summary

Upon completion of the *felt needs* exercise you will have a well-defined sense of what you _feel_ is important in your life. This powerful gut-level sense speaks to your audience's feeling level, and acknowledges an understanding of their existence by telling the truth of your own existence. Such insight gives speakers an open-mindedness that enables them to disclose what they know of their own truths. This type of honesty awakens speakers' vulnerability and leaves an audience free to examine their own truths.

When you successfully identify yourself with what you need, want, and desire, your message becomes the platform for examining the felt needs we all have in common.

This concept is of utmost importance in a HeartTalk because it allows speakers to examine how they process what they think and how they feel. Digest this information, relate it to your topic and it will provide a powerful method of communicating the complexities of how needs affect judgment, behavior and strategy.

Speaking Out Loud

Take two minutes to stand and orally practice explaining how your needs affect your judgment, behavior, and strategy in relation to this topic. To familiarize yourself with thinking on your feet, speak as your thoughts occur to you. Don't be concerned with moments of silence; just remember to either keep speaking or processing information for the full two minutes.

Values And Conflicts

"The greatest and most important problems of life are all in a certain sense insoluble....They can never be solved but only outgrown," ~ C.J. Jung.

Great athletes are able to consistently overcome failures, disappointments, and rejections, because the focus and development of their talents are not governed by internal conflicts, but by inherent values. Conflicts, for such people, are indicators that they have lost sight of what is worthwhile. Conflicts are never an issue for those who are aware and connected to the excellence they mean to express. Values have the power to erase conflicts, neutralize fear and rebuild self-reliance.

Values have the power to erase conflicts, neutralize fear and rebuild self-reliance.

The intention of a HeartTalk is to focus on the topic in such a way as to allow each member of the audience to identify values and harmonize conflicts pertaining to the speaker's subject matter. HeartTalks remind listeners to reclaim their values by focusing on what is worthwhile, instead of investing too much time in attempting to solve their problems.

No matter how far removed they may seem from the speaker's message, all conflicts and all values are connected and universally common. Hence it follows that the speaker must first identify the values and conflicts of his own life.

For example, all failures, disappointments and rejections - no matter what caused them - may create conflicts that deprive people of their happiness, peace of mind, and self-worth. Such conflicts might impair one's ability to concentrate by focusing time, talents and resources on the conflict instead of what is important, e.g., poise, fulfillment, and personal excellence.

No matter what the circumstance, these conflicts and corresponding values are universal and inspire thoughts that help listeners regain self-assurance and direction.

A HeartTalk recognizes and addresses universal values and conflicts. Listeners benefit when the speaker's message draws refreshingly larger insights that allow the listener to experience greater clarification, growth, and freedom. Both listeners and speakers, with their conflicted mental obsessions, personal values, and life experiences, seek inner resolution and integration.

Certain thoughts and feelings, such as loyalty conflicts, self-consciousness, fear of loss, and feelings of envy can restrict the fulfillment of felt needs. Thus, these issues, identified along with the other values and conflicts, require new ways of thinking to bring them into a more productive mindset.

Some speakers try to sidestep their own internal values and conflicts by using trite and hackneyed excuses. For instance, when a speaker gives a "head talk," personal conflicts or values are rarely mentioned and, often, the speaker's clichéd reasons misdirect the attention of the audience by focusing on, say, blaming, exaggerating, and minimizing, instead of examining. Speakers who utilize this strategy deprive listeners of the opportunity to identify their own internal thought processes. When the message strays from the speaker's values, his message ultimately weakens, because condemnation forces listeners to take sides— instead of taking heart. Political positions assign burden, while heart positions accept the responsibility of inspiring new ways to think.

To identify your values and conflicts, complete the **Values and Conflicts** exercise on the following page. Read the directions carefully, and make sure you time yourself accordingly. When completed, move to the next page, and continue.

Values and Conflicts Exercise

Take a sheet of paper and list the three things most important to you. Then list at least two things in conflict in your mind, or in your direct experience. Your lists do not have to be related to your topic.

Values

1. Example: *I value my friends, and experience.*

2.

3.

Conflicts

1. Example: *I have problems at work that seem to defy my solutions.*

2.

3.

Summary

A speaker's personal values and conflicts are powerful because they represent issues that can be examined without accusation. Speakers who seek to probe and cease to blame can make real progress toward the creative concepts necessary for productive change. When you speak with the authority and candor of your own values and conflicts, you do not have to apologize for your position. This removes the highly-defensive *"prove-it-to-me"* attitude of some audiences, helping to open up many listeners' minds to grasp the speaker's message.

A speaker who has not identified first-hand values and conflicts relative to the topic fails to communicate a message of the heart. Such failure forces the speaker to take the position of having to persuade, rather than inform and enlighten. Speakers who address their own values and conflicts relative to a topic always have a better chance of communicating their message to a larger number of individuals. Many people tend to mindlessly endure conflict and pain, repeatedly using the same excuses to avoid change. This will probably always be true of many of the members of your audience. Your HeartTalks will help those listeners face their conflicts and identify their values.

Combining <u>direct experience</u>, <u>felt needs</u>, and <u>values and conflicts</u> creates the possibility for an expanded level of communication. A HeartTalk must begin and follow through with this type of honesty. To speak from the heart, one must establish this kind of authenticity and communicate the validity of direct experience, the presence of felt needs, and the reality of personal values and conflicts. Audiences yearn to hear the voice of conviction. HeartTalks are powerful because they begin with the **Voice of Authenticity**—a position that is believable and based on a genuinely-felt truth!

Audiences yearn to hear the voice of conviction.

37

Speaking Out Loud

Stand, take three minutes, and orally practice surveying your values and conflicts, relating them to the topic. Speak as your
thoughts occur to you and do not be concerned with trying to fill every moment with
words. Thinking as you speak will require
some brief pauses. Remember to continue
for the full three minutes, and feel free to
include information from previous exercises.

3

The Glue that Holds It Together

Joseph Campbell, author of the *Power of Myth,* referred to myths as *"masks"* that give meaning and stability to our understanding of life. Central to all religions, myths enable cultures to find the common attributes that give order to their existence, in much the same way purpose provides a framework for a HeartTalk.

Speakers who reveal the influence of their authenticity will more likely command the attention and respect of their audience. But that respect will fade quickly, and lose meaning, without a well-defined purpose for the presentation. **Purpose** gives a speaker stability, and is an essential part of a HeartTalk. Purpose is the invisible quality that holds your thoughts together. A well-prepared message utilizes purpose by organizing it according to a mental structure that keeps it on course as the speaker presents her point of view. **Purpose** then becomes the energy of a HeartTalk.

Purpose is the invisible quality that holds your thoughts together.

41

No matter how enthusiastic a speaker is, without purpose she risks rambling into uncertainty and losing the focus of her talk. On the other hand, even a mediocre talk can be kept upright if it has a clear purpose. This way, wandering or missing the point is less likely to occur. Purpose, therefore, clarifies and substantiates the message being delivered. It is the glue that holds a HeartTalk together.

Purpose promotes stability because it is based on the **state of mind** a speaker seeks to create, the **actions** a speaker wants to occur, and the **results** the speaker is seeking. Purpose never insists on audience response, but conveys unquestionable knowledge of the topic. This stability allows speakers the freedom to explore and examine, without getting lost, any and all subject matter. This type of stability can set a speaker free to develop a delicious sense of spontaneity, keeping the audience excited about where the speaker is going and how she is going to take them there. To further understand **purpose,** let us examine its

42

three primary components: **state of mind, action, and results.**

State of Mind

When a famous professional golfer was asked the secret of his exceptional putting ability, his reply was simply: "You have to want to sink it." In a HeartTalk, the desire to be, do, or have is created by your **state of mind.**

Everyone has a state of mind centered on something to *be, do,* or *have.* If people want to be, do, or have something enough, their minds immediately start to create the feeling of what they want. The more you desire something, the more your desire dictates your behavior and, hence, the more you will (knowingly or unknowingly) conspire to have what you want. Therefore, a state of mind will either govern or be governed by the demands of what you want to be, do, or have.

A HeartTalk's purpose is to focus on creating a state of mind that will help the listener to transform her own desires into stimulated feelings and inspired thoughts. A well-determined, heartfelt state of mind binds the speaker to the message, thereby linking the listener to that state of mind in which the speaker is absorbed. Such reflection represents the inner intensity of purpose. It is the state of mind to which the speaker's thoughts and emotions become attuned, and to which an audience responds. This intensity - or vibrancy - is a dynamic component of a HeartTalk because it gives the speaker's message an invisible energy, form, and power, without losing the relaxed and casual manner of her delivery.

For this reason, Speaking From The Heart can never be faked. Audiences know when a speaker is inspired because they feel the honest intensity of her state of mind. Therefore, **state of mind** is essential to a HeartTalk because it neutralizes self-doubt—the primary cause of self-consciousness and the fear of public speaking. Doubt

44

cannot exist when the speaker knows what she needs to learn in order to think more productively, and to experience more directly the benefits of her message. Once a speaker knows the state of mind she is aiming for, it becomes easy to link thoughts and emotions together into energetic words, phrases, and thematic ideas.

To identify the state of mind a HeartTalk seeks to create, the speaker must ask the kinds of questions that confront whatever needs to change within the speaker's heart. The answers to these questions then communicate what the heart wants to experience, e.g., freedom, confidence, safety, security.

To get in touch with the state of mind necessary to communicate your message, complete the **State of Mind** exercise on the following page. Read the directions carefully, and make sure you time yourself, accordingly. Then continue on.

State of Mind Exercise

Take a sheet of paper and answer the following questions. Be as spontaneous as you can, putting down anything that comes to mind. Give yourself about three minutes per question to do this exercise.

Topic: _____
(Sample: Breakdowns, Freedom and Goals)

1. What do I need to learn about myself that would help me become more receptive to my topic? <u>Example</u>: *Why I keep reacting to breakdowns as though they're not supposed to happen.*

2. What state of mind would help me create a more productive attitude about my topic? <u>Example</u>: *Less rigid, more flexible. Not so self-critical or self-abusive.*

3. What could I have, that I don't have now, that would provide me with a more direct experience in relationship to my topic? <u>Example</u>: *Courage to push barriers, greater awareness of potential breakdowns, greater confidence to handle my freedom.*

Summary

Once you have established the state of mind your message will convey, your intellect automatically starts to organize your thoughts around a clear and vivid mentality, resulting in words of confidence and strength.

The state of mind a HeartTalk creates now attracts the audience to new possibilities, empowering listeners to integrate the value of the speaker's ideas into their own lives. Therefore, the state of mind awakened by what a speaker knows must change in her own life helps listeners confront the changes they know must happen in their lives. Speakers who seek to control listeners' minds, instead of sharing what is in their own hearts, always run the risk of becoming superficial, while HeartTalk speakers come across as real.

State of Mind attracts the audience to new possibilities

Speaking Out Loud

Stand, take two minutes, and orally practice reviewing the details of what you know
you must be, do, or have in order to fully
understand your topic. Speak as your
thoughts occur to you, and don't be alarmed
if there are vast stretches of silence.

Just because a speaker is silent does not
mean her audience, or her mind, has
stopped thinking. Think of your words and
thoughts as pebbles tossed into a deep pool.
Silence depicts the natural amount of time
it takes for the speaker's ideas to sink in.
Speak and think for the full three minutes.
Do not apologize nor make excuses for your
silence.

<u>Action</u>

Action turns the crank of a HeartTalk and,
like an alarm, calls the fire engine to the
fire. A HeartTalk has the power to crank
and/or alarm; therefore, a speaker must

always consider what her state of mind is asking the audience to do. Action is the work the message suggests, the new aim in life guided by thought and attention. Part of the aim of a HeartTalk is to redirect the listener's attention to a more productive way of thinking, hence a more productive mode of acting.

Action is the new aim in life guided by thought and attention.

For example, if your aim is to work more positively with difficult people, the action you take may be to neutralize your personal judgment of someone's negative behavior which, in turn, enables you to talk to the person, instead of reacting to the unfavorable behavior.

Listeners, however, may have a multitude of reasons and habits that, consciously or unconsciously, make it difficult to take the new actions necessary to achieve more productive outcomes. Some reasons: *my family has always been overweight and poor; my 5th grade teacher told me I have no talent for that; I'm too old; I'm not educated.* Speakers must therefore create powerful and logical rationales to help motivate listeners to take the necessary actions to erase the emotional, mental, and physical barriers that have limited their results.

Speakers must give listeners new ways to think, to help stimulate the concept of new actions. If the way is clear, and the logic is in place, HeartTalks provide listeners with information that redirects their behavior toward productive utilization of time, energy, resources, and feelings—much like a ship changes direction in response to weather reports.

The action a HeartTalk speaker shares must be a real account of her own experience if she intends to inspire others to take action in their own lives. Listeners yearn to know how the speaker corrects her own behavior, and what strategies she used to change her attitude or emotional responses regarding the topic's related issues. This is an important part of a HeartTalk's purpose - and must be clearly thought through - in order that the speaker's corrections, methods and responses can be shared in an open and honest manner. Genuineness is lost if this information is exaggerated or minimized.

Observations that appeal to a more elevated or effective way of disciplining one's thoughts can reveal how frequently and unconsciously we compromise the possibility for a more productive life. Most often these subliminal compromises are driven by states of mind that are no longer useful or necessary, but nonetheless linger in our subconscious memories thereby influencing the activities of our lives. These states of mind might include prejudice, resentments, abuse, jealousy, and a speaker who is willing to share such encounters as related to the topic, gives listeners a valuable gift—opportunity to examine the actions of the speaker and to begin to mentally imagine a new course of action for themselves.

To identify the action called for in your message, and to specify your subconscious limitation—as related to the topic, complete the **Action Exercise** below. Read the directions carefully, and make sure you time yourself, accordingly. When completed, continue to the next exercise.

Action Exercise

Take a sheet of paper and answer the following questions, as honestly as possible. Don't hold back anything that may seem too painful or risky to examine. Remember, this material is <u>for your eyes only</u>.

1. List at least three activities that are called for in your topic. <u>Examples</u>: *To know my goals and how to implement them; To change the way I handle breakdowns; To not be frightened by my freedom.*

2. List between one and three ways you tend to compromise your desires when it comes to this topic. <u>Example</u>: *I avoid success because it means more responsibility and less freedom, and breakdowns give me an excuse to fail.*

3. List two mental, physical and emotional demands implied by your topic.

    Mental Examples:

    a. *I have to be patient...stop reacting to my breakdowns.*

    b. *Try to remember the benefits of achieving my goals.*

    Physical Examples:

    a. *To exercise and rest, in order to keep focused.*

    b. *To schedule carefully, avoiding overwhelm.*

    Emotional Examples:

    a. *To identify and neutralize my fears.*

    b. *To acknowledge every success, no matter how small.*

Summary

One of the most beneficial parts of a HeartTalk is the examination of the new actions your subject matter suggests, compared to any of the mental, physical, or emotional demands that might compromise or limit your newly-defined behaviors. For example, my lack of patience and poor scheduling compromises my desire to effectively accomplish my goals.

HeartTalks stimulate listeners to think, and what listeners think often stimulates a conflict between the new thought and the old habit-driven action. This comparative examination helps audiences develop new ways of thinking. These new ways of thinking are best described if they are a part of the speaker's examination of her own limitations, as related to the topic. In addition, once the speaker knows exactly what actions need to change, and why, she can begin to eliminate the need for notes.

Such information is easy to remember because it is emotionally and intellectually personal to the speaker's own life. Creating HeartTalks reveals new information to the speaker about compromises, new activities and old beliefs. This is why every HeartTalk feels fresh, original and spontaneous, empowering speakers to demonstrate a genuine enthusiasm for what they have to say.

Information is easy to remember because it is emotionally and intellectually personal to the speaker's own life.

Speaking Out Loud

Stand, take two minutes and, without stopping, orally review all of your notes on action. Speak spontaneously, as your thoughts occur, and explore the meaning of what you know must change in your actions. Contrast what you know must change, with what you believe causes you to currently resist such changes. Don't worry about extended pauses; remember to think and speak for the full two minutes.

Results

Regardless of your intended goals, the results an audience achieves will vary on each occasion, and often clash with *"what was supposed to happen."* Speakers must clearly convey the goal of their message; otherwise, listeners cannot grasp the intended results.

When this happens, listeners often discard good ideas when they can't picture themselves experiencing or applying the result. A listener may think, "Good idea, but what has it got to do with me?" An audience's needs can only be satisfied when the listener can clearly see that the result is of direct benefit.

Paradoxically, a HeartTalk never promises a specific result but, rather, a greater experience of the benefit. To do this, the purpose must have an ideal reward—a practical benefit applicable to the listener.

The intention of a HeartTalk is to direct the listener towards an action, thought, or idea that can be internalized to help them achieve a better way to think, yet leaves them free to realize their own result.

To establish the ideal benefit of a purpose, a HeartTalk must simplify complex ideas and generalize any details that tend to overwhelm. The end results must move the listener toward a revelation, confident of finding a fulfilling experience.

To help generalize and simplify your desired results, complete the **Results Exercise** on the following page. Read the directions carefully, and make sure you time yourself accordingly. When completed, continue on to the next exercise.

Results Exercise

1. On a sheet of paper, list three to five general results each member of your audience will achieve by assimilating your suggestions. Keep desired results brief, and plausible for everyone. <u>Examples</u>: *Lose the fear of breakdowns; Experience more freedom, and less tension; Review and frequently update goals; Change my attitude about the action of success.*

2. Now, list three to five simple ideas contained in your message. These ideas should be no longer than seven words each. <u>Examples</u>: *Goals and perspective cannot be fixed, only changed; Breakdowns are symptomatic of a need to know; Confronting fear is necessary for growth; Goals are what you try to achieve; Vision is what you grow into.*

Summary

Results are a primary part of **purpose** and must be well-secured in the speaker's mind. Although you may never refer to these directly, your audience will intuit your own awareness of the results you have in mind.

Results help to clarify a speaker's message, making it safe and easy for audiences to examine their own goals as they relate to the topic. Now, complete the following exercise labeled **The Purpose of My Message**.

The Purpose of My Message Exercise

Using the information from the completed exercises in this chapter, write three short, sentences that powerfully describe: (1) the **state of mind** your message conveys; (2) the **action** it requires; and (3) the **result** you want. Remember, the intent is to simplify the complexities of your message and direct your listener to a new and beneficial way of thinking, acting, and living.

Example: *The purpose of my talk is ...*
State of Mind: *Identify why some choose failure over freedom.*
Action: *Provide a practical model for living through breakdowns.*
Results: *Greater freedom, peace and personal power.*
Speaking Out Loud

Stand, take six minutes, and orally practice reviewing the **purpose** of your talk. Without notes, examine what you can remember about the **State of Mind** that led you to your **purpose**. Reflect on what you have decided is necessary to for you to learn, solve and/or explore in order to achieve the results your message suggests. Question the **action** your topic seems to imply, as if you were seeking to persuade someone who is uncertain of the practicality of such behavior. Address old beliefs that need to be changed because they compromise your freedom and success. Pique the curiosity of your make-believe audience by briefly describing the changes you've made in your own mental, physical and emotional life. Analyze the results your message promises to achieve, and help your audience see how these results have transformed the way you think.

Do not worry nor be concerned with extended periods of silence. Thoughts and silent reflection are important components of a HeartTalk. Seek to address your audience in a spirited but casual manner, as if speaking to your best friend, eager for them to understand the ideas and concepts you have recently learned, discovered and/or applied.

The opening of a HeartTalk includes the following information: who the speaker is; her **purpose** for being there; the **topic** she wants to address; the **felt need, direct experience**, and **values** and **conflicts** that compel her to talk. If you are a beginner, a good way to start is by saying, "My name is... My topic is... The purpose of my message is... A direct experience that stimulated my curiosity... What I have discovered... What I need to learn..."

4

Where are We Going with This?

Interactive Elements

Occasionally, audiences question where a speaker is headed with his point. This is a problem only if the speaker has the same doubt. The difference between the thought process of someone who knows where he is going, and someone who does not, is in the clarity of the speaker's **vision**, **intention** and **desire**. **Vision** maps the destination. **Intention** fuels it with passion. **Desire** drives it home.

HeartTalk speakers use these **interactive** elements to provide listeners with current data essential for meaningful change. Vision, intention and desire are fundamental to human nature, hence facilitate the process of uniting listeners with speakers, playing on the affinity between the direction of the speaker's message and the destinations listeners crave.

Interactive Elements link listeners to transformational concepts.

HeartTalks inspire change by using interactive elements that link listeners to transformational con-

65

cepts. Breaking down barriers, beliefs and old excuses, these ideas are immediately useful in guiding listeners past their fears. **Vision, intention** and **feelings** elevate and quicken the positive imagination of listeners' minds, broadening their capacity to understand.

Interactive elements help speakers interpret and translate the universal and internal language of feelings. A listener's apathy is easily converted to effective action when the speaker's message clarifies the meaning and power of one's feeling.

Corresponding principles that lead and link listeners to objectives more readily appear when the **direction** of a HeartTalk is clear in the mind of the speaker. Speakers who heed the interactive elements of their messages will enlighten listeners, while heartening their enthusiasm to see the advantages of a new pathway of thought. When such direction comes from the heart, speakers feel natural and genuine, never forged nor phony.

This kind of communication strengthens confidence in listeners' minds because it helps them to internalize new and more enthusiastic points of view. For example, speaking on the importance of the Red Cross, a speaker's intentions might be to link his audience to an emotional identity, helping them grasp the feeling of what the Red Cross does. Reporting or editorializing on its features will not create the empathy necessary to link the audience to the organization.

In a HeartTalk, speakers form these links by probing their own interactive connections to the subject. To better understand the terms vision, intention, and desire, examine their definitions and apply their qualities.

Vision

A speaker's clear vision makes it easy for listeners to see the advantage of the speakers point of view. Clear vision defines the benefits of a message and provides a degree of intensity that must be genuinely felt by, and personally relevant to, the speaker. The benefits of a speaker's message, however, are not always easy to identify because they tend to be confused with features—the facade or image of what something does versus the result of its existence. For instance, describing the features of the Red Cross may explain its importance, but will not activate a sympathetic link within the listener. However, a personal story of the Red Cross' lifesaving response to a disaster will join listener and organization in an emotional bond, leaving "not a dry eye in the house."

The benefits of vision are the anchors of meaning audiences hunger for and use to initiate and strengthen the resolve neces-

68

sary to change the way they think and live. Benefits are powerful because they are the practical results of what you're talking about—the insight that easily compels someone to take action.

A further example of the two might be the wonderful feature of the blood-gathering capability of the Red Cross and how it saves thousands of lives each year. Seen as a benefit, one would have to tell a story. A story, perhaps, that allowed a child to be raised by a parent that might have died if it wasn't for the blood and emergency services of the Red Cross.

The feature is the systems and programs that gathered and delivered the blood. The benefit, however, is the emotional energy of those life-changing events that instantly put all other problems into perspective, transcending processes and systems by delivering messages of hope and meaning. Systems and programs might be interesting, but children and families are *compelling*!

Speakers find the guidelines of their vision in the spirited atmosphere and mental structure their topic suggests. To extract these powerful stimulants, imagine and describe the emotional environment your subject matter predicts. To understand this process, think of yourself as a witness, testifying at a trial about new insight that dramatically clarifies and changes the perception of the jury.

How would this NEW environment or structure benefit you and/or the people around you? What would it add to your life that is not already there? What old ideas and emotions would it neutralize or erase that are still in direct conflict with how you want to behave, think and/or feel? HeartTalk speakers use the answers to these questions to attract listeners into a state of genuine probability. The subject matter of a HeartTalk invariably points to new modes of thought, feeling and behavior.

To create the visual benefits for your subject matter, complete the **Vision Exercise** which follows below. Be sure to allow yourself enough time to identity the benefits and the feelings they forecast.

Vision Exercise

Take a sheet of paper, fill in your topic and take three minutes per question to do this exercise. If you get stuck and can't think of an answer, improvise.

TOPIC: _____
(Sample: Breakdowns, Freedom and Goals)

1. Briefly describe the new emotional environment your topic suggests:
   Example: *A calm mind that directs the rationale necessary to make productive choices.*

2. Briefly describe the new mental attitude or structure your topic suggests:
   Example: *A stronger conviction that strengthens my ability to achieve my goals.*

3. Briefly describe the benefit these changes represent to yourself:
   Example: *I have a much clearer idea of what I intend to do and want to achieve. It is easier to explain my desires.*

4. Briefly describe the benefit this topic suggests to those around you:
   Example: *People around me find it easier to know how to help and I find it easier to say more definitely what I can and cannot do for them.*

5. Briefly describe the new points of view this topic proposes:
   Example: *Life is not as hard when you're clear. People are happier when they know what to say yes and no to.*

6. Briefly describe what conflicts are neutralized or erased as a result of the ideas generated by this topic:
   Example: *The indecision of not being sure of what I really want; New feelings of expectancy that are more powerful than my old fears.*

Summary

In the early 15th century, Portuguese sailors navigated the oceans of the world, in part by observing and recording the color, flow and conditions of the sea. While other sailors wandered aimlessly, the Portuguese knew what to look for and what to do when conditions changed. Vision provides speakers the same advantage.

Vision communicates the emotional, mental and physical benefits of where a HeartTalk is going. Identified in your answers, these focal points become the tangible landmarks listeners learn to recognize and recall when, and as, they encounter the conditions that require them to change the direction of their lives. Hence, HeartTalks give listeners a tremendous advantage—the knowledge of how to get to where they want to go when conditions change. Such knowledge not only guides listeners to the benefit of the speaker's message, it becomes a benefit in and of it-

> *Vision communicates the emotional, mental and physical benefits of a HeartTalk*

self by mapping the mental oceans listeners will travel over and over again.

Later, this information will help in the selection of stories, poems and anecdotes so indispensable for accurately describing, and thus impressing upon the listener's memory, the essential attributes and subtleties that navigate their lives.

Speaking Out Loud

Taking three minutes, stand and talk casually, explaining the emotional, mental, and physical landmarks that will guide listeners to your intended destination. Be as graphic as possible in describing these landmarks. An interesting exercise is to imagine your listener is blind. If you must stop and think for a moment, keep in mind silence is an indication to listeners that you are genuinely being thoughtful concerning your message. *HeartTalk Proverb: "Thinking requires contemplation...the thoughtful regard for what one is saying."*

74

Intention

Intention is the fuel of passion that enables listeners to feel the energy of speakers convictions. For example, Christopher Columbus left port with the intention of finding a new route to India. He was convinced the world was round and thus his felt need to discover a new passage called him to take action—irrespective of the fear and superstition felt by the majority.

Intentions start within every person as felt needs that are well-defined and call for specific actions. However, these actions will gradually become unconscious, monotonous and redundant if they come from the memory of a person's repetitive needs. That is, what we *tend* to do when certain ideas, situations or conditions stimulate us to recall the _feeling_ of the need. Reinforced by enough experience, intentions will, over time, become automatic and invisible to the average person as the reason for a behavior. Many people will deny

Intentions start within every person as felt needs.

75

unconscious intentions are the cause to their reactions. However, for most, behavior is an attribute of impulse caused by habit, and every habit or impulse was first an intention. Somewhere in your <u>direct experience</u> (the last 24 hours) of life your habitual intentions reveal themselves. The objective of a HeartTalk is to motivate the desire within the listener to change his behavior with new and well-defined intentions.

If a speaker wants his audience to adopt a new mental attitude he has to create desire by having the passion for it himself. Without such passion a speaker cannot link a listener to a greater understanding. He can only give them an overview of the features and report on the good it's seems to do, e.g., *"Tell me something I don't know."* A speaker may increase the listener's desire to understand, but he will not motivate listeners to change their intentions/behaviors until he illustrates how and why his own intentions have changed. Intentions fuel the passion of a message essential for stimulating the listener's interest. This must be unquestionably apparent in the speaker's conviction. To clarify intention complete the **Intention Exercise** below. Allow plenty of time to answer the questions, then continue.

Intention Exercise

On a sheet of paper answer the questions below. Don't hold back any information that appears too painful or risky to examine. Remember, this material is <u>for your eyes only</u>.

List at least three common reactions you personally observe in yourself or others when you talk about this topic.

Write in your topic: _____
(Sample: Breakdowns, Freedom and Goals)

1. <u>Example</u>: *Freedom is what I want, after I finish my work.*
2. <u>Example</u>: *Breakdowns are too painful, even if it is the only way to freedom.*
3. <u>Example</u>: *Goals are too limiting. They require too much work. Besides, ambition is not spiritual.*

List at least one common reaction you used to have, but have since changed when it comes to this topic.

1. Underline: Example: *My freedom was not as important as my sacrifice.*
2. Underline: Example: *Goals are more important than people.*
3. Underline: Example: *Breakdowns are abnormal.*

Using the information from the previous exercises, write three sentences stating the intentions you now have towards your topic.

1. Underline: Example: *Freedom is as powerful a driver of human behavior as sex.*
2. Underline: Example: *Every goal achieved will eventually lead to a breakdown.*
3. Underline: Example: *Breakdowns must be redefined and perceived as a necessary step in the evolution of human development.*

Summary

When you share the evolution of your intentions, explaining the how and why of your changes, listeners' feelings of well-being expand. Intention is a powerful interactive element that provides new insight from which listeners' can see the possibility of their potential—a new criterion for making choices. Plainly defined, intentions outweigh and erase the old reasons for habitual behaviors that have caused many of the unexplained and illogical reactions listeners frequently experience, but are unlikely to admit.

Later, in the chapter on research, you will utilize your defined intentions as criteria for selecting stories to stimulate feelings that help audiences change their intentions with regard to your topic.

Speaking Out Loud

Taking three minutes, stand and talk casually, explaining the how and why of your new intention concerning your topic. Share as much detail as you can, but remember to keep talking for three minutes. If you can't remember everything during your three minutes, simply be quiet, rethink the details and share more as it occurs to you. The silence all speakers encounter during the delivery of a speech is a normal aspect of communication. Though sometimes awkward at first, listeners and speakers eventually welcome moments of silence in a talk because they mark the end of a thought, and allow the opportunity to consider what is being spoken.

Some methods treat the pause as a tool speakers insert for dramatic emphasis—re-sist this temptation! In a HeartTalk, the pause is a NATURAL part of how words and ideas flow. The heart knows when to be silent. Only the ego, undirected by the heart, would try such a TRICK, and listeners can detect what is real/meaningful and what is dramatic/entertaining. *HeartTalk Proverb: Seek not to make pauses happen, rather, allow them to happen.*

<u>Desires</u>

"My prayer is to linger with you, at the end of the day..." These words, borrowed from an old 50's rock'n roll ballad, accurately describe the interactive desire many people have to be loved. Audiences respond to such desires because it compels them to remember what is really important—the things that make life worthwhile.

HeartTalks reflect similar desires. Audiences are compelled to listen to speakers who can remind them of what they really want. Such desires are the hidden persuaders that draw listeners onto the pathway of a speaker's thoughts. Correctly identified, interactive desires mirror and magnetize the feeling nature that mo-

Interactive Desires mirror and magnetize listeners' feeling nature.

81

tivates listeners to want to grow. It is the same tool advertisers use to sell the sizzle/ effect a product promises. Hence, speakers must identify the desires that will drive and compel listeners to the new actions their topics suggest.

Desires are best described as words and concepts that deliver the feeling of the speaker's message. Without such feelings, listeners may grasp the importance of what is being said, but never be attracted to the action the topic calls for. On the other hand, speakers who get carried away with their own feelings forget to deliver the message, much like a sales person who forgets to ask for the order.

Think of it this way: a hungry person who orders a pizza doesn't care who brings it. Hungry people only know they are hungry. Conversely, listeners know the hunger/desire of their hearts and crave ideas and answers that might satisfy that desire. They don't care who brings them the message as long as what they want is delivered.

Desires empower and magnetize the content of a message. However, desires must be carefully matched to the idea. The message must carry a desire that emotionally agrees with its content. Hence, listeners will readily accept an idea the moment they're convinced it can satisfy their desires, give them what they want, or take them to where they want to go.

To find the desire most useful and capable of attracting the listener to the message, a speaker must think of the desires responsible for the changes in his own actions. Think of how it feels to have the advantages of your new desires. Contrast the new desires with the old, and describe the evolution of those desires. Use words that communicate the *sensation of what you desire*. Well-written movie reviews in newspapers or magazines can give you some great ideas for words and phrases designed to motivate people to go and see a movie. However, people don't go to see words. People go to see movies because the words stimulate the desire and attract the listener to the action. Still, desire is not the action—it is what motivates and guides the action. HeartTalk speakers must find words that echo the sizzle of the desire, guiding listeners to a new action, a new way to think.

Use the words suggested in the **Desires Exercise** below to describe the feeling of what you want to say. Be creative and add as many of your own words as you wish. You can't do this wrong!

Desires Exercise

Circle the words below that best represent the feelings and thoughts that drive your opinions about your topic. Take a sheet of paper. Using these words, and/or any other words that occur to you, write one to three sentences that describe the feelings generated by your topic. Write these sentences as if your topic was a movie you were urging a friend to go see. You can't do this wrong!

Elite, Alert, Qualified, Blast, Surplus, Replay, Ecstasy, Lethal, Acoustic, Hollow, Paradise, Shocking, Mystery, Invasion, Master, Chilling, Fun, Scary, Genuine, Unnerving, Suspenseful, Ultimate, Tension, Winner, Debut, Learn, Energy, Primal, Fatal, Hilarious, Romantic, Riveting, Displaced, Rampant, Doubt, Alternative, Beginners, Rage, Species, Sloppy, Special, Spice, Magical, Original, Faster, Clever, Independent.

Sample Topic:
Breakdowns, Freedom and Goals

Example: *Breakdowns are **genuine** and sometimes **unnerving**. The feelings of freedom that from time to time result from breakdowns can be cause to a **primal blast** of emotions that **alerts** the senses to new and **original** data. Goals, however, can be washed away in a flood of **raging data, displacing** conformity and confidence with **doubt** and **tension**.*

85

Summary

Desires are the hidden persuaders that make a subject sizzle with interest and energy. When you see a movie or play you like, you talk about it in a way that usually makes others want to see it. A HeartTalk speaker has the same type of enthusiasm. Learn to use words to describe characters, plot, tension, surprise, structure, the things you learned, how it entertained, or how it changed you. Your exuberance is a catalyst for interest. Your emotional effervescence can electrify listeners creating the desire within them to want to know more.

Speaking Out Loud

Taking three minutes, stand and talk about your topic as if it were the best movie you have ever seen. Share as much detail as you can, and remember to keep talking for three minutes. Use the words and ideas from the desire exercise. Stay natural in your delivery, but allow yourself to express as much excitement as possible. Listen to the intensity of your voice, and experiment by raising and lowering its volume.

5

Research

One of the key components of every HeartTalk is the information that supports a speaker's position. Many speakers, unfortunately, struggle over what to take out and what to leave in. The information they've gathered all seems relevant to, and necessary for, their presentation, but there simply is not enough time to include everything. In addition, the amount of time spent in outlining, categorizing and analyzing tends to sap energy from the speaker and thus diminish her enthusiasm. Research done in this manner is far too intellectually draining and time consuming.

HeartTalk research is different because it follows a guide that is **intuitive** rather than intellectual. The intuitive guide is directed by felt needs that simplify the search by acting as internal criteria, telling the intellect what is important and truly relevant, rather than what is simply related to the topic. Research and composi-

*HeartTalk research follows a guide that is **intuitive** rather than intellectual.*

tion must be fun, quick and direct if they are to energize the speaker and raise her enthusiasm.

Because HeartTalks come out of an awareness of one's direct experience, felt needs, values, and conflicts, research for a HeartTalk speaker is **ongoing**. If you tell your mind to index your experiences of joy, conflict, resolution and need, your mind will remember the details of how you have felt, reacted and lived within your own direct experience. All of these will guide your intellect in previewing and selecting information that is directly suitable for your HeartTalk.

Research, guided intuitively, is fun and easy. Your intuition quickly eliminates what is not relevant to the topic and acts as a magnet that draws all that is necessary to communicate and justify your position and purpose.

HeartTalks seek to illuminate where ignorance has prevailed, to pinpoint information that can free people from repressive behavior, and to open listeners' minds to the benefit illustrated by the speaker's point of view.

Research is a necessary part of a HeartTalk, but it must be a natural part of the gathering of information as the speaker forms new opinions and discovers fundamental ideas. If you allow intuition to lead the way, you will easily browse through the information around you to identify what is **directly relevant**. If you allow intellect to lead the way, you will gather information relating to your topic, but not necessarily relevant to it.

Allow intuition to lead the way, to identify what is directly relevant.

93

Written Material and Other Media

Books, magazines, newspapers, TV and radio shows are great sources for a HeartTalk. But given the considerable number and variety of media, a speaker must be able to quickly preview and gather only information that is directly relevant to her topic. An intuitive search must be easy, quick, and directed by the purpose and voice of authenticity. Complete the exercises allowing plenty of time, then proceed the next section.

How To Research Books and Magazines

With your topic, purpose and voice of authenticity in mind, allow yourself to visually examine, in a casual manner, the covers and titles of books and magazines in libraries and bookstores. <u>Do not try to choose something specific, **rather,** allow your intuition to discern what is pertinent.</u>

The picture on the cover, the title, or even the shape and design of a book or a magazine will call you to it. IT MAKES NO DIFFERENCE IF THE TITLE DOES NOT APPEAR TO HAVE ANY DIRECT RELATIONSHIP TO YOUR TOPIC.

Remember, your intellect is biased and will always relate to something it already knows. The heart, however, is always open to any source of information that will nurture understanding. New material will, of course, be related and relevant, but in a manner the intellect could not have imagined.

TITLE OF PUBLICATION:

_____

1. Briefly describe in one sentence why this publication appealed to you.

2. Briefly describe in one sentence what you think this publication's content will address.

3. After you have read the last page, first page, and index, skim the last sentence of each paragraph in each section/chapter and list three to five facts or ideas revealed to you. Write your revelations in short, clear statements. This exercise should take no more than ten minutes. If the book is too long skip a chapter or section. Just make sure you get your three to five points.

TITLE OF MAGAZINE & ARTICLE:

_____

1. Briefly describe in one sentence why this article appealed to you.

2. Briefly describe in one sentence what you think the content of this article will address.

3. After you have read the last paragraph and the first paragraph, list three to five facts or ideas this article has revealed to you. Write your revelations in short, clear statements.

How to Research Radio, Movies and TV

With your topic, purpose and felt needs in mind, allow yourself to remember the last TV, picture, or radio show that caught your attention. **Do not search for specifics**, rather, **allow something to occur to you**. Again, IT MAKES NO DIFFERENCE IF THE SHOW DOES NOT APPEAR TO HAVE ANY DIRECT RELATIONSHIP TO YOUR TOPIC. You are looking for new and fresh connections to your topic.

TITLE OF RADIO, TV SHOW OR MOVIE:

_____

1. Briefly describe in one sentence why this show appealed to you.

2. Briefly describe in one sentence what you think this show's content addressed.

3. Briefly tell of this show's story and include its primary characters, its plot and conclusion.

Composition

Upon completion of the exercises in this chapter, you will be ready to **compose** the first part of your talk. Composition, like research, must be fun, easy and quick if it is to have the kind of enthusiasm necessary for a HeartTalk. Therefore, open with a clear message that identifies:

1. who the speaker is;
2. his/her purpose;
3. the topic;
4. the felt need, direct experience, values and conflicts that compel the talk;
5. the benefits envisioned;
6. a little about the research and ideas guiding the desired message.

Delivering The First Part of Your Message

INSTRUCTIONS:

1. Write your topic in the center of the mind map on the following page.

2. Start your talk by telling your audience your name and topic.

3. Using this guide, speak for six minutes touching on all four areas, sharing as much as possible.

4. Do not use any other notes. Speak only from memory.

5. If you run out of things to say, simply wait in silence until something occurs to you.

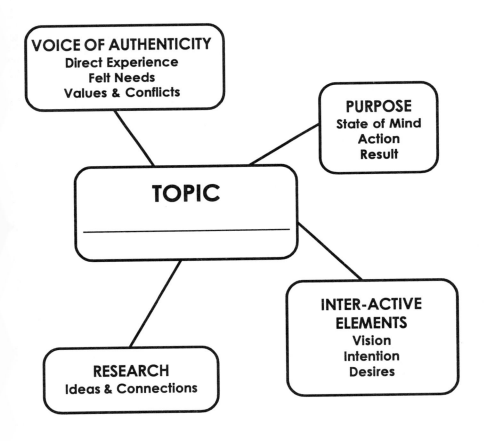

6

Tools
of
Composition

When you have something to say, HeartTalks work. The whole key to speaking without notes is to personalize your material and your topic so you become spontaneous in what you say, yet disciplined in how you say it. To understand this freedom, you must practice in order to gain the experience of running into a moment's wall of silence. You will soon learn to accept this lapse without panic and ease back into a HeartTalk delivery.

The key to speaking without notes is to personalize your material

If you will allow it to happen, your mind will draw a picture from your heartfelt imagination, feelings and dreams, and it will paint that picture using logic, metaphor, story, humor and words. Together, your feelings and mind can extract the essence of what you want to say from the ideas, concepts and thoughts stimulated by your heartfelt needs, direct experience, values and conflicts. This will be the body of your talk, and once you get used to your mind "thinking on its feet," so to speak, you will be amazed at how much fun and freedom you will begin to experience. To feel this freedom you must carefully read the sections on tools, and follow the directions in the exercises. This may seem time consuming at first, but after a while these tools will start to work for you **while** you're delivering the message. There are five basic tools a speaker must learn to use to deliver a HeartTalk:

LOGIC: organizes and categorizes important information. Logic emphasizes the power and capacity of your intellect and seeks its cooperation in support of understanding where the heart is leading you.

STORY: illustrates the feelings, intent, and benefit of your message.

METAPHOR/SIMILE: uses poetry, comparisons, and analogies describing the function, nature, and mechanics of how the speaker's ideas work in life.

106

HUMOR: points the way, by relaxing and opening your audience to new, joyful adventures in listening.

WORDS: draw attention by stimulating your interests and challenging your habits of language and thinking.

Logic

The logic of any HeartTalk must answer two questions: (1) "How can this talk help the speaker to understand life?" and (2) "How can ideas in this message change the speaker's life?" The moment you (the speaker) ask yourself these questions, your intellect will immediately start to analyze, weigh, compare and measure what is already known or assumed. In so doing, it usually starts to identify problems and create solutions all at once. A solution-oriented talk, on the other hand, while possibly satisfying to a speaker's intellect, is rarely relevant to the listener's heart. A listener's reaction to such a talk might be characterized by the statement "You may be right, but who cares?"

What the heart of the listener is waiting to hear is more closely allied with abstraction. That is, the essence or key ideas suggested by the speaker, rather than the solutions typically stimulated by analysis. Such key ideas can unlock the attention of the audience, giving both listener and speaker permission to go deeper into the meaning of their lives and thus expand their concepts of how life can yield greater benefits for them. Abstractions bypass the barriers of culture and tradition and can help both speaker and listener release expectations or prejudicial thinking.

That being said, an important distinction must be drawn between the analysis and the abstraction of a topic. While a HeartTalk seeks to free the heart of the listener by sharing new and creative key ideas (abstractions), the speaker must not forget that the egocentric nature of many listeners tends to reject a speaker who totally ignores the conventional wisdom most often associated with solving problems. Most listeners require some amount of logical analysis directed towards problem solving in order to calm the self-absorbed nature of their intellect.

A HeartTalk must feed both the intellect and the creative appetite of the listener. It must consistently instruct the listener's intellect to acknowledge, but not measure, its self-worth. A HeartTalk must define the benefit of its presence.

A HeartTalk must feed both the intellect and the creative appetite.

It must avoid the self-critical nature so often voiced by the intellect's response to anything new, i.e., the devil's advocate. A speaker's logic must never seek to control the listener; it must seek to inspire, teach and unite. To understand the power of logic, please turn to the next page and complete the **Mechanics of Logic Exercise.** When you are finished, go on to the following page and continue.

Mechanics of Logic Exercise

There are two ways to apply logic to your topic. The first and most common way is to analyze your topic by fragmenting it into problems, with solutions that provide new findings. The second and least understood way is to generalize or abstract the essence or key ideas your topic represents, creating a new basis for activities or ways of thinking. The logic of any HeartTalk must include both analysis and abstraction. It must help the listener to understand new ideas and to make changes that are beneficial and constructive.

Complete the following exercises.

1. Reduce your topic to one or two problems, and provide easy to understand solutions. <u>Example</u>:

<u>Topic</u>: Breakdowns, Freedom, and Goals

<u>Problems</u>: Breakdowns can severely disrupt emotional stability and productivity. Escape is often mistaken for freedom.

<u>Solutions</u>: See breakdowns as normal. They are part of a common and healthy trial-and-error process that provides new and important decision making data. The solution to escapism is to more closely monitor your emotions before you react. All of humanity is socially and culturally programmed to react. No one escapes the mind's tendency toward snap opinions. However, you can train your mind to acknowledge your emotions without resorting to toxic conduct.

2. Abstract one or two main ideas to which your topic draws attention. <u>Be careful these ideas are not problems</u>. Strive to make these similar to observed scientific phenomena. <u>Example</u>:

   <u>Topic</u>: Breakdowns, Freedom, and Goals
   <u>Ideas</u>: Goals should be short-termed, measurable, achievable, and a part of an overall fluid vision. Freedom, however, is not a goal. Freedom is an inherent quality/feeling that you cultivate—not achieve, measure, or justify.

3. Describe a point of view opposite of your solution or observations. This is important, because your audience will automatically start to polarize and compare what you're saying to what they know. <u>Example</u>:

   <u>Topic</u>: Breakdowns, Freedom, and Goals
   <u>Common Opposing Views</u>: I have always been told that my first reaction is the right reaction. Freedom is something you earn for good behavior.

Story

The purpose of a story is to illustrate, and lead the mind of the listener toward, the feeling of what is being communicated. Thus, a HeartTalk story does more than tell—it stimulates the emotional memory of speaker and listener. Stories always have meanings that underlie their literal message and provide a foundation for telling the truth. They speak to all people and

A HeartTalk story stimulates the emotional memory of speaker and listener.

make it easy for the listener to explore private, often concealed, feelings. In Clarissa Pinkola Estes' book, *Women Who Run With The Wolves*, seventeen stories use individual characters to represent the collective behaviors and attitudes of human cultures. These analogies expose generalized patterns or models of human conduct termed ***archetypes***—prototypes or examples containing vital information about human behavior, helpful for understanding how life works.

HeartTalks tell stories that reflect archetypal patterns that help listeners go deeper into their understanding/ experience of the subject matter.

For example, in Estes' telling of the story *Skeleton Woman,* she likens the fate of a young woman killed by her disapproving father to the destruction of the creative spirit of young women by men collectively.

In his book *Iron John,* Robert Bly tells the story of a forest in a kingdom into which various types of people enter never to return. The archetypal forest represents a state of mind that perceives life as so dark and dangerous, we think we will disappear if we venture too far or too deep.

Robert Fritz, in his book *The Path of Least Resistance,* alludes to the way streets in Boston are confusing because they follow the cow paths of earlier settlements. This narrative expresses a common pattern of

114

thinking, i.e., how our minds may, like cows, follow the path of least resistance.

In the sample topic, Breakdowns, Freedom and Goals, the attitudes, archetypes and patterns from these stories are quite applicable. Breakdowns can have the feeling of the forbidden forest. Freedom is sometimes threatened by "lazy cow path" attitudes. Goals can be easily compromised by destructive cultural patterns.

Drawing new connections, and comparing and contrasting archetypes through the telling of stories, enlivens subject matter and makes the delivery of a HeartTalk easy and fun. Once in a while, students in my class will question the importance of stories. People everywhere want to hear stories because stories contain information about the heart and how it desires to express itself in the world.

My friend Mark Victor Hansen and his partner, Jack Canfield, have proven the tremendous interest people have in stories. Printed in twenty languages, their book *Chicken Soup For The Soul* has sold millions of copies; succeeding *Chicken Soup* titles have grown into a popular series.

I like to use stories from the *Chicken Soup* books in many of my presentations because they always point to what matters most in the hearts of my listeners. HeartTalk stories work, because stories can safely expose listeners to their hidden feelings. Unless exposed, hidden feelings can usurp all logic sustaining the deadly attitudes that need to change in order to live a more productive life.

The key to telling an analogous story is to find how the characters, circumstances, and/or environments compare to the generalized patterns or archetypes of human behavior, conditions, or attitudes. The beauty of this is that all stories that unveil universal archetypes are applicable to any topic. Bly's forbidden forest, Fritz's cow path topography, and Estes' skeleton

116

woman can fit any topic because the archetypes are universal. Are there not dark forests, "cow path" thinking, and the effects of destructive attitudes in all of us? Even the most mundane talks about statistics, software, or urban freeways, for example, can draw brand new parallels when a speaker can point to the dark forests, cow paths, or cultural attitudes comprised by his subject matter. To understand the power of a story, please read the example below, then complete the **story** exercise immediately following.

"The Window"

Taken from *A 2nd Helping of Chicken Soup for the Soul,* by Jack Canfield and Mark Victor Hansen.

There were once two men, both seriously ill, in the same small room of a great hospital. Quite a small room, it had one window looking out on the world. One of the men, as part of his treatment, was allowed to sit up in bed for an hour in the afternoon (something to do with draining the fluid from his lungs). His bed was next to the window. But the other man had to spend all his time flat on his back.

Every afternoon when the man next to the window was propped up for his hour, he would pass the time by describing what he could see outside. The window apparently overlooked a park where there was a lake. There were ducks and swans in the lake, and children came to throw them bread and sail model boats. Young lovers walked hand in hand beneath the trees, and there were flowers and stretches of grass, games of softball. And at the back, behind the fringe of trees, was a fine view of the city skyline.

The man on his back would listen to the other man describe all of this, enjoying every minute. He heard how a child nearly fell into the lake, and how beautiful the girls were in their summer dresses. His friend's descriptions eventually made him feel he could almost see what was happening outside.

Then one fine afternoon, the thought struck him: Why should the man next to the window have all the pleasure of seeing what was going on? He felt ashamed, but the more he tried not to think like that, the worse he wanted a change. He'd do anything! One night as he stared at the ceiling, the other man suddenly woke up, coughing and choking, his hands groping for the button that would bring the nurse running. But the man watched without moving—even when the sound of breathing stopped. In the morning, the nurse found the other man dead, and quietly took his body away.

As soon as it seemed decent, the man asked if he could be switched to the bed next to the window. So they moved him, tucked him in, and made him quite comfortable. The minute they left, he propped himself up on one elbow, painfully and laboriously, and looked out the window.

It faced a blank wall.

Story Exercise

1. Briefly describe, verbally, the characters and their universal tendencies.

2. Briefly and verbally describe the setting.

3. Try telling the story to yourself in 90 seconds.

4. Briefly describe, orally, how this story relates to your subject matter and your life.

5. Does the story have confusion or conflict you can compare to anything currently happening in your life?

Take a sheet of paper and list three to five thoughts you have uncovered about yourself and your subject matter from this story.

Simile/Metaphor

A metaphor is the expression of one idea that veils another. For instance, if I said "you are a butterfly, fluid and whimsical, but subject to the wind," I have used a metaphor. But if I compared your behavior to that of a butterfly using the words *like* or *as*, I have used a figure of speech called a simile. The use of similes is found throughout all great literature because they stimulate the heart into responding artistically and creatively. When you use such tools to reflect your own observations of how life tends to work, you can safely expose yourself and your feelings without distracting your audience with unnecessary emotions.

To practice using similes, look around for something that attracts your attention. It is best to choose a mechanical or biological thing rather than a person. Select something from your immediate environment. Write a short statement about how it works, and an equally short statement of the function it performs.

121

Now, combine the two into a brief description of how it relates to life. Upon completion of the task, you may be surprised at the profound lesson contained in your new analogy.

To understand the power of metaphor and simile please complete the **Simile Exercise** below. When you are finished, go on to the next page and continue.

Simile Exercise

1. Choose an object, and describe it.

2. What is it?

3. How does it work?

4. What does it do?

5. How does it relate to real life? My life is like a _____ because...

Example:

Sample Topic: Breakdowns, Freedom, and Goals

1. *I am looking at a universal remote control.*

2. *It is a device used to control the functions of a TV, VCR, or Stereo.*

3. *It sends an electrical signal.*

4. *It can change channels, adjust volume, play back, rewind, and skip tracks.*

5. *My life feels like a universal remote in the hands of a stranger. It changes conditions without my permission, skips ahead without my knowing, and plays back my emotions just when I thought I was past that problem. Sometimes its signal is misused in fractured attempts to control behavior, results, and/or impressions.*

Humor

Most everyone has a sense of humor. However, some humor reflects a jaded sense—hostile in intent and delivery. HeartTalks know the danger of this kind of humor; its intent is to find fault or ridicule; it expresses a kind of criticism that exploits and judges. Such humor may gain the attention of an audience, but it will do little to inspire them to anything heartfelt.

In order to understand the kind of humor used in a HeartTalk you must eliminate the notion that such humor is about telling jokes. While the well-placed joke may enhance a point, the kind of humor I am talking about is a sort of stand-up joy, rather than of stand-up comedy. The process seeks to communicate and share the joy the speaker has found in his own life, for the purpose of relaxing the audience, while removing their guard. Seeking to share the experience of joy through humor is inclusive to all. Seeking to exploit or criticize through humor forces the audience

124

to decide whether or not they are included in the humor or have become the object of the humor. Even the slightest hint of cynicism can raise the listener's guard and thus prevent the arrival of your message's intent.

Speakers who have decided to give a HeartTalk must cultivate their own awareness and expression of joy and spontaneity. They must endeavor to remember the small, kind pleasures of the day and use their newly-discovered joy to relax and disarm their audience. A HeartTalk speaker doesn't worry about whether what he says is funny. If the words captured the speaker's sense of joy, the audience will feel the accompanying delight.

As you find more joy and share it, your collection of stories and insights will multiply, and so will your happiness. To experience the power of humor complete the **Humor Exercise** on the following page. Then continue on.

Humor Exercise

List one to three experiences of joy you can remember, that relate to each of the following categories:

PEOPLE

PLACES

CONDITIONS

WORK

Words

Thoughtfully selected words are stimuli for new and creative thinking. Choose words to serve your purpose. If you choose words for their "showiness" you are likely to misdirect your audience. Words are like spices in food. The combination of spices can create a new taste. Thus, words will blend and create new tastes and appetites.

Since numerous words are loaded with multiple meanings, a HeartTalk speaker knows that their contextual use of a word may not be what the audience is used to hearing. Therefore he must define, with confidence, the purpose and direction of his meanings. That confidence will stimulate and be felt intuitively by the audience so they can safely take their minds down new pathways of thinking.

To build your vocabulary, pick out five new words from a book, magazine or newspaper and begin to add those to your repertoire. Adding new words on a continual basis will help keep a speaker out of the sea of sameness. Experimenting with new words will transform what you have to say into a more specific and interesting talk. To understand the power of words please complete the **Words Exercise** on the following page.

Words Exercise

Write down the definitions you think best apply to the list of words below.

Incumbent

Lust

Officious

Peculiar

Read a movie review or a concert review. Take a sheet of paper and list two to five words that draw your attention from the review. Use those words to describe your direct experience of life over the last 24 hours. Combine the words from the review with the four above and see if you can use them all in orally describing or explaining your subject matter.

Example:

Topic: *Breakdowns, Freedom, and Goals*

Sample Review: *Taken from an opera review in the* Los Angeles Times, *written by Mark Swed.*

"L.A. Opera has climbed up into the attic and blown the dust off an old relic to begin the new fall season. Yet—stroke of fate—it was an old relic that seemed newly relevant..."

Sample combination: *Long term goals seem like incumbent demands keeping us away from the relevant importance of our fate. Like lust-filled adolescents, however, we instinctively sneak up to the attic of human emotions and dust off our peculiar history hidden by officious attitudes that deny feelings, desires, and past experiences.*

7

Presentation and Delivery

Presentation

The whole key to speaking without notes is in how you personalize your message to yourself. HeartTalks work because they have something to say. Speaking without notes is not about memorizing, it's about knowing exactly what you want to say.

Your two most powerful tools are your **interactive heart** and your **directive mind**. The mind uses logic and words to explain the point of view. The heart uses simile, metaphor, stories and humor to demonstrate the benefit of the message. Together, they paint pictures of true feelings while drawing connections to real needs, thereby provoking your audience to *consider* a possible change in their individual behaviors and thinking—a change that will benefit them and help them to live a more productive and positive life.

A HeartTalk is artistically constructed around your authenticity, purpose, and direction. If these components are personal

133

and clear in your own mind, your HeartTalk will create itself. Your intellect must never dominate your thinking. You must learn to use the intellect's ability to measure, weigh and compare in order to direct your message as it flows from your lips, while allowing your heart to be its inspiration and guide.

Plotinus, an early Greek philosopher, believed there are three ways we gather and share information: science, opinion and illumination.

Science deals with our powers of observation, and discovery of the laws of nature. Science tells us of reoccurring phenomena that can help us utilize life for productive and constructive purposes. In a HeartTalk, science can help us illustrate how things appear to work.

Opinion can help us gain new understanding of how things work using different points of view.

Typically, most people gather and share information in this manner. In a HeartTalk, opinion can help explain an experience from differing points of view. However, the speaker must be careful to be respectful of all points of view or run the risk of neutralizing the purpose and intent of the presentation with a cynical distraction.

Illumination spontaneously reveals dynamic information that is a part of our felt need and direct experience. It is intuitive because it provides information that comes from a broad and deep sense of who we are versus what we have learned, read, or seen. It is an important key to understanding our relationship to the topic, because it reveals a cultural and personal motive for our behavior. In a HeartTalk, illumination can evenly tie our own preferential point of view to a broader point of view more inclusive of the listener.

The delivery of a HeartTalk involves a combination of reports, observations and analysis, examining other's opinions and drawing new connections to make change possible.

HeartTalks are authentic expressions of who we are, where we are in the growth process, and how the passage is working for us. HeartTalks have a spontaneous quality, both revealing and creative. HeartTalks flow in the direction of the speaker's purpose and always seek to direct the listener to examine and clarify her own feelings.

HeartTalks are motivated by the knowledge that every word out of your mouth is guided by a positive expectancy and collective benefit. Audiences are hungry for the authentic. They anticipate and await great discoveries, revelations and benefits.

Delivery

A HeartTalk is different from a speech. Speeches are given; HeartTalks are delivered. By changing your concept from giving to delivering, you can change your whole mental and physical sense of what you are

> Speeches are given; HeartTalks are delivered.

doing. This will **relax** you and help you step away from the pedestal effect that giving speeches tends to create.

If you stand in front of a large crowd and think to yourself, "I am here to deliver a message," it's like telling an audience, "I am here to deliver the pizza." Like any good speaker (chef), you've assembled your message (pizza) and prepared an interesting (tasty) combination of purpose, authenticity and inner active elements (sauce). Your stories, logic, humor, similes and words give rise to a whole new experience of listening (dining). Your felt needs identify your unique qualifications and help to distinguish you from other speakers (chefs).

137

If, on the other hand, you stand in front of a large crowd and you think to yourself, "I am here to try and give a speech," it's like telling your audience, "I am here to share with you how others and I have tried to make pizza in the past." If your audience was hungry, they would listen to your explanation with effort and maybe even identify with your problem, but would go unfed.

Speakers who give speeches are perpetually worried about preparation, acceptance, and the value of what they have to say. Do I have enough to say? Will they get what I am saying? Will they laugh at my jokes? Will I remember the punch lines?

The delivery person differs because she has confidence in her product. Her preparation and cooking have already been done. Calmly, and joyfully, she simply serves the message knowing that it is genuine, authentic, and original. Her stories are like the freshest ingredients because they come from her direct and most recent experience. Her logic is tantalizing because it has created a whole new refinement in the way we think. Her words snap us out of our indifference and open us up to whole new dimensions of feeling and action. Her interactive direction moves us to feel intellectually fed and emotionally nurtured.

HeartTalks flow from opening, to body, to close. Follow the directions for each part. Allow yourself one page of notes, and put it away. If you need to, take out the page, unfold it and once reminded, put it away. Remember, notes held in your hands can distract you.

Directions For Opening

1. Write your topic in the center of the mind map on the following page.

2. Make sure that you start your talk by telling your audience your name and topic.

3. Speak for six minutes touching on all four areas, sharing as much as possible.

4. Do not use any other notes. Speak only from what you can remember.

5. If you run out of things to say, simply wait in silence until something occurs to you.

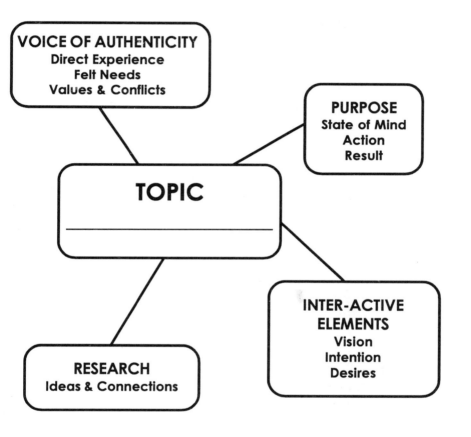

Directions For Body:

1. When you've clearly established your topic, purpose, need, and ideas move to the body of your talk.

2. At first, start with your logic, and share your observations, abstractions, analysis and conflicts.

3. Share some stories that compliment your logic... sprinkle in some metaphors and joy.

4. Use your research to help keep you focused on your purpose and vision (benefit).

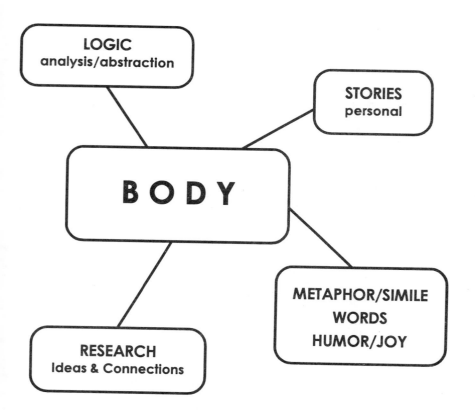

Directions For The Close

1. Write your opening topic in the center of mind map on the following and fill in the closing topic (conclusion).

2. Review your original purpose and vision, and share how it has changed your behavior and beliefs.

3. Ask your audience to join you in considering a change or a possibility.

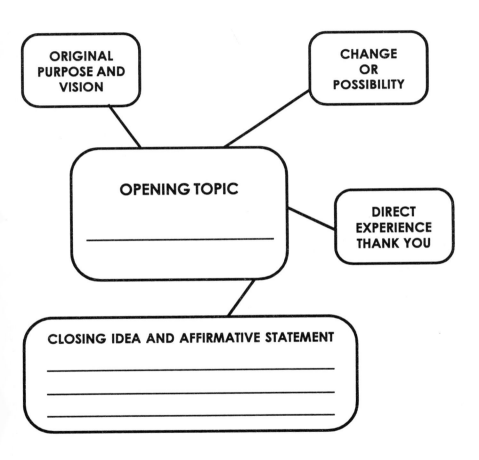

8

Summary: Putting It All Together

To compose effective HeartTalks in a short period of time:

1. Establish your **topic** and then, in one to three complete sentences, set your **purpose** in mind.

2. Keep track of your **joy**, and the **stories** you've read or heard. Monitor your **direct experience**, **felt needs**, **conflicts**, and **values**.

3. Approximately two to three hours before your scheduled talk, prepare your message. Start by reviewing your **current position, topic** and **purpose**. Be sure and walk around and do most of your composing on your feet or on the move. Limit yourself to one piece of paper and keep your notes brief and symbolic. As you think about your **logic,** tell your mind to remember or recall **stories**. To

jog your imagination and jump-start your creative sense, start making up **similes** based on things close at hand. As you envision the **benefits** of your point of view, jot them down in one or two words. Stay relaxed and don't try to force this process.

4. As you learn to trust your heart, it will provide all the information you need to give a warm, personal and inspired presentation.